Bilingual Edition
READING POWER
Edición Bilingüe

Cobi Jones

Soccer Star

Estrella del fútbol soccer

Rob Kirkpatrick

Traducción al español
Mauricio Velázquez de León

The Rosen Publishing Group's
PowerKids Press™ & **Buenas Letras**™
New York

1

To the teachers who made school fun.
A los maestros que hicieron divertidos mis estudios.

Published in 2002 by The Rosen Publishing Group, Inc.
29 East 21st Street, New York, NY 10010

First Bilingual Edition 2002
First Edition in English 2001

Book design: Maria Melendez

Photo Credits: p. 5 © Ken White/Allsport; p. 7 © Jamie Squire/Allsport; p. 9 © Brian Bahr/Allsport; p. 11 © Stephen Dunn/Allsport; p. 13 © Rick Stewart/Allsport; pp. 15, 22 courtesy of UCLA Sports Information Department; p. 17 © Aubrey Washington/Allsport; p. 19 © Jonathan Daniel/Allsport; p. 21 © Ken White/Allsport.

Text Consultant: Linda J. Kirkpatrick, Reading Specialist/Reading Recovery Teacher

Kirkpatrick, Rob.
    Cobi Jones : soccer star = Cobi Jones : estrella del fútbol soccer / by Rob
Kirkpatrick : traducción al español Mauricio Velázquez de León.
        p. cm.—(Reading power)
        Includes index.
        SUMMARY: Introduces Cobi Jones, star player for the Los Angeles Galaxy
            soccer team.
        ISBN 0-8239-6135-4
            1. Jones, Cobi Juvenile literature. 2. Soccer players—United States
Biography Juvenile literature. [1. Jones, Cobi. 2. Soccer players. 3. Spanish
language materials—Bilingual.] I. Title. II. Series.
        GV942.7.J66 K57 1999
        796.334'092—dc21
        [B]

Word Count:
English: 120
Spanish: 133

Manufactured in the United States of America

Contents ────

──── Contenido

Cobi Jones plays soccer.

———

Cobi Jones juega
fútbol *soccer.*

Cobi plays for the Los Angeles Galaxy.

———

Cobi juega con Los Ángeles Galaxy.

7

Soccer players kick the ball to move it. This is called dribbling. Cobi likes to dribble.

Los jugadores de fútbol usan los pies para hacer avanzar el balón. A esto se le llama driblar. A Cobi le gusta mucho driblar.

The ball can go in the air. Then Cobi can hit it with his head.

———————

A veces el balón se eleva en el aire. Entonces Cobi puede golpearlo con la cabeza. A esto se le llama cabecear el balón.

Cobi plays soccer all the time. He even plays when it is wet and cold.

———

Cobi juega *soccer* todo el tiempo, aunque llueva o haga frío.

13

Cobi went to school at
U.C.L.A. He played soccer
at U.C.L.A.

———————

Cobi fue a la Universidad
de California en Los
Ángeles (U.C.L.A). Jugó
fútbol en el equipo de su
universidad.

Cobi has played for the United States team.

———————

Cobi ha formado parte de la selección de los Estados Unidos.

17

Soccer players can get
tired when they play.

———

Los jugadores de fútbol
soccer se cansan
mucho en los partidos.

Cobi is happy when he scores a goal. He runs around when he scores.

———

Cobi se pone feliz cuando anota un gol. Corre alrededor del campo cuando anota.

Cobi loves soccer.

———

A Cobi le encanta
el fútbol *soccer*.

Here are more books to read about
Cobi Jones and soccer:
Para leer más acerca de Cobi Jones
y fútbol soccer, te recomendamos
estos libros:

Cobi Jones: Soccer Games
by Cobi Jones, Andrew Gutelle,
illustrated by Paul Meisel
Workman Publishing (1998)

Soccer Game! (Hello Reader!)
by Grace MacCarone, illustrated by
Meredith Johnson
Scholastic Trade (1994)

To learn more about soccer, check out
this Web site:
Para aprender más sobre fútbol
soccer, visita esta página de
Internet:

http://sportsline.netscape.com/ns/
soccer/index/html

23

Glossary

dribble (DRIH-bul) When a soccer player moves the ball with his feet.

goal (GOHL) When a player puts the ball in the net and scores a point.

team (TEEM) A group of players.

Index

Glosario

anotación Conseguir un gol para tu equipo.

driblar Cuando un jugador de soccer hace avanzar el balón con los pies.

equipo (el) Un grupo de jugadores.

gol Cuando metes el balón en la portería del otro equipo.

selección (la) Equipo que representa a un país en competiciones internacionales.

Índice